"HERE MEN FROM THE PLANET EARTH
FIRST SET FOOT UPON THE MOON
JULY 1969, A.D.
WE CAME IN PEACE FOR ALL MANKIND"

NEIL ARMSTRONG

NEIL ARMSTRONG
Space Pioneer

Paul Westman

Lerner Publications Company ■ Minneapolis

ACKNOWLEDGMENTS: The photographs are reproduced through the courtesy of: pp. 1, 2, 6, 12, 19, 21, 24, 25, 27, 29, 30, 31, 32, 34, 35, 37, 38 (top and bottom), 39, 40, 41, 42, 45, 47, 48, 49, 51, 53, 54, 55, 56, 57, 59, 61, 62, National Aeronautics and Space Administration (NASA); pp. 8 (top and bottom), 23, Smithsonian Institution; p. 13, North Carolina Department of Commerce; p. 15, Purdue University News Service Photo; pp. 16 (top), 17, U.S. Naval Institute; p. 16 (bottom), National Archives.
Front and back cover photographs by NASA.

To my father, Bert F. Westman, who loves flying
almost as much as Neil Armstrong does

LIBRARY OF CONGRESS CATALOGING IN PUBLICATION DATA

Westman, Paul.
  Neil Armstrong, space pioneer.

  (The Achievers)
  SUMMARY: A biography of Neil Armstrong who, on July 20, 1969, as a member of the three-man Apollo 11 crew, became the first human being to walk on the moon.

  1. Armstrong, Neil, 1930-   — Juvenile literature. 2. Astronauts — United States — Biography — Juvenile literature. [1. Armstrong, Neil, 1930-   2. Astronauts] I. Title. II. Series: Achievers.

TL789.85.A75W47   629.45′0092′4 [B] [92]   80-10832
ISBN 0-8225-0479-0 lib. bdg.

Manufactured in the United States of America

International Standard Book Number: 0-8225-0479-0
Library of Congress Catalog Card Number: 80-10832

5 6 7 8 9 10 90 89 88 87

NEIL ARMSTRONG

July 24, 1969. Everyone had waited anxiously for this day to come. In the Pacific Ocean southwest of Hawaii, a rescue ship had been ready for hours. Soon a helicopter began hovering over the blue green ocean. Swimmers in black rubber suits moved restlessly in the water, staring up into the clouds.

Suddenly someone saw a dark spot in the sky, far off. Then the *Apollo 11* spacecraft came rushing toward the rescue crew, with huge parachutes billowing out behind it. Minutes later the spacecraft splashed safely into the ocean. The waiting was finally over. People throughout the world heard "Splashdown! Apollo has spashdown!" on their televisions and radios.

After their successful splashdown in the Pacific Ocean, the three astronauts (seated in the raft) were flown by helicopter to the U.S.S. *Hornet.*

The president of the United States had come halfway around the world to congratulate the three men who were now bobbing in the ocean. After all, this day had made history. Commander Neil Armstrong and his crew had just returned from the moon!

Practically all his life Neil had been preparing for such a historic trip. Yet he never would have guessed it as a boy. Neil was born August 5, 1930, on his grandfather's farm in northwest Ohio. The closest town, Wapakoneta, was surrounded by woods, rolling hills, and rich farm land.

When Neil was only two years old, his father took him to see the air races in Cleveland, Ohio. Mr. Armstrong boosted Neil up onto his shoulders, high above the crowd. As the planes roared by overhead, little Neil clapped his hands and laughed in delight. He was thrilled at how fast the brightly painted planes could go. Many years later, Neil decided it must have been then when he fell in love with flying.

Besides the city of Cleveland, Neil saw many other towns in Ohio. Neil's father worked as an auditor for the state government. He traveled from county to county, examining records to make sure that officials used money honestly. Because of his work, the Armstrongs often had to move. They lived in the towns of Warren, Jefferson, Havana, St. Marys, and Upper Sandusky. Finally, though, the Armstrongs moved back to Wapakoneta, where they bought a house and settled down for good.

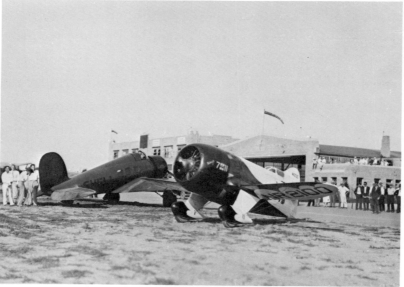

Neil was only two years old when he attended the 1932 Cleveland
National Air Races with his father.

The Armstrongs were a close family who attended church regularly. Neil, his sister June, and his brother Dean all did their share of work around the house. They mowed the lawn, weeded the vegetable garden, and helped with the laundry.

While Neil was still quite young, his mother spent hour after hour reading to him, and he learned to love books. Neil read 90 books when he was in first grade! He skipped second grade completely, for by that time he could read as well as fifth graders.

Although Neil met a lot of other kids at school, he did not make friends easily. He had always been quiet and shy. He did play football and baseball with the other boys, but most of all he liked building model airplanes.

Neil first became interested in models after his first plane ride when he was six years old. His father took him to a nearby airport, where they climbed into a small plane called a Tin Goose. They began to taxi slowly down the runway. Then the plane picked up speed and lifted into the air.

Soon they were soaring high above Wapakoneta and the surrounding countryside. It seemed to Neil that the town was made of toy houses, and that tiny cars moved up and down the streets. Neil was more amazed when he realized that the little specks were people! As the plane headed away from Wapakoneta, Neil looked down at the checkered fields. Their patterns looked like one of his mother's patchwork quilts. And the winding river gleamed in the sun like a blue satin ribbon.

By the time they landed, Neil was eager to learn more about flying and the machine that took people so high above the earth. He went to a hobby store and bought a few model airplane kits. At first he put together simple models powered by rubber bands. Soon he was building more complicated ones using wood and wire. During the next few years, Neil made hundreds of model planes. He even built many small airplanes from scratch, using whatever materials he found around the house.

When Neil finished one of his models, he would test it in the grassy park near his house. Curious youngsters gathered to watch. They could not understand why Neil's planes always flew faster and farther than their models. The reason was very simple. Neil put more effort into making his models than the other children did.

He even built a wind tunnel in the basement of his house. The wind tunnel had a fan to blow air through it. Neil placed different models in the tunnel to see how well they would fly. Then he chose the designs that worked best.

Neil's interest in experiments showed up in school as well. He particularly liked science and mathematics. It was not long before he had learned everything in his science and math textbooks.

One of his teachers, Mr. Crites, helped Neil go on to more difficult studies. He learned calculus, a complicated form of math. Neil also began to read about astronomy. He thought stars and planets were almost as fascinating as airplanes.

One of the Armstrongs' neighbors, Mr. Zint, owned the most powerful telescope in Wapakoneta. Often he let the neighborhood kids look at the night sky through the powerful lens. Most of the children took their turn at the telescope and then wandered off to play, but Neil looked and looked at the twinkling, mysterious sky. He saw the rings of Saturn and the red planet of Mars. He also gazed at the moon. Because the moon was closer to the earth than the stars and planets, Neil could see it in much greater

Years after studying the moon through a small telescope, Neil became the first person to walk on the moon. This photograph of the moon was taken from *Apollo 11*, 10,000 miles away from the moon's surface.

detail. In fact, the moon seemed so close that Neil felt he could almost reach out and touch it.

As he grew older, Neil never lost interest in the sky and flying. He collected and studied issues of *Air Trails*, a magazine about flying. He filled notebooks with scraps of information he found on different airplane makes and designs. Neil especially enjoyed reading about the Wright brothers. In 1903 Orville and Wilbur Wright had made the first motor-powered plane flight in history. They had grown up in a town not far from Wapakoneta.

Neil decided that he, too, wanted to be able to fly a plane someday. But first he had to take lessons, and they cost nine dollars an hour! So he began to do odd jobs around town whenever possible. He

When Orville and Wilbur Wright made their famous flight on December 17, 1903, their small plane traveled 120 feet and stayed in the air for 12 seconds.

worked in a bakery, a hardware store, a grocery store, and finally a drugstore. By the time he was 15, Neil had saved enough money to take flying lessons. The day he first soloed, or flew alone, was one of the most thrilling moments of his life. Then, on his 16th birthday, he received his student pilot's license—even before he had his driver's license!

Neil had worked hard to save enough money for flying lessons. But he knew he would have to work even harder to earn enough for college. After all, he could not expect his parents to pay his way completely. Neil had read about how the United States Navy offered college scholarships to people who were willing to join the service. It seemed like a good way to pay for school, so Neil applied.

One day during his senior year in high school, Neil got a letter in the mail from the navy. The letter said that he had been awarded a scholarship. In return for his schooling, Neil had to agree to serve whenever the navy wanted him.

In the fall of 1947, Neil entered Purdue University in Indiana. He had completed two years there when the navy ordered him to Pensacola, Florida, for flight training. Neil became a naval air cadet.

The Purdue University campus in the 1940s

The Korean War broke out in 1950 while Neil was still at Pensacola. The navy sent Neil and many other pilots to fight in Korea. Neil was the youngest man in his unit.

During the war, Neil flew 78 combat missions.

During the Korean War, Armstrong piloted a Navy Panther jet.

On one mission, a cable stretching across a North Korean valley clipped the wing of his Panther jet. Neil coaxed the crippled plane back over friendly territory before bailing out. His courage and flying ability won him the respect of his comrades aboard the U.S.S. *Essex*, the aircraft carrier that Neil was stationed on, and the navy honored him with three air medals.

The U.S.S. *Essex*

After Neil left the navy in 1952, he went back to Purdue to finish his degree in flight engineering. In his spare time, he taught math courses and delivered the campus newspaper to earn money. While delivering papers one chilly morning, he bumped into a pretty, dark-haired girl, Janet Shearon. It turned out that she knew a lot about flying herself. Neil and Janet discovered they had many other things in common and began to see each other often. They were married in January 1956.

After college Neil went to work as a research pilot at the Lewis Flight Propulsion Laboratory in Cleveland, Ohio. While he was there, his interest in space flight grew. He told one of the directors at the laboratory, "I think space travel will someday be a reality. When it is, I'd like to take part in it." Few people would have dared to make such a bold prediction in 1955.

Soon Neil took another job as a test pilot at Edwards Air Force Base in California. Most of the other pilots lived in the town of Lancaster, but Neil and Janet bought an old cabin overlooking a beautiful valley in the nearby San Gabriel Mountains. The cabin, which had once belonged to a forest ranger,

An aerial view of the Lewis Flight Propulsion Laboratory (later called the Lewis Research Center)

had no hot water or electricity. The Armstrongs worked hard to restore it.

They also kept busy with their two children, Ricky and Karen, who were born during these years at the base. Karen died from a brain tumor when she was only three years old. A second son, Mark, was born later.

In spite of the tragedy of Karen's death, the years at Edwards Air Force Base were some of the happiest of Neil's life. Much of his time he flew airplanes. Being a test pilot was dangerous work. The planes Neil tested flew faster than the speed of sound. Several times he had close calls. But Neil loved the adventure and excitement of flying and doing important research.

Two of the most interesting planes he flew were the X-1 and X-15 rocket planes. Each was actually half-rocket and half-airplane. They were designed to fly into the fringes of the earth's atmosphere. This was the closest human beings had come to space travel.

Neil flew the X-15 to speeds of 4,000 miles per hour and as high as 40 miles. Neil was flying almost as high as his plane could go. To go any higher, he would have needed a spaceship. From that altitude the view was much like what astronauts would later see from outer space. The earth even looked round from that height. People on the ground were awed by the sight of Neil flashing through the sky in the X-15. "He flies an airplane as if he's wearing it," one admirer said.

Armstrong, a civilian test pilot for NASA from 1952 to 1962, often flew the X-15 rocket airplane.

Neil became one of the best pilots in the world while working at Edwards Air Force Base. But he was an engineer and experimenter as well. He flew planes to learn more about aircraft design and performance. He contributed much to the development of new methods of flying.

The United States was not the only country experimenting with different forms of air travel. Its biggest rival, the Soviet Union, launched the first satellite into outer space in 1957. Every 96 minutes the satellite circled around the earth. At times it was as far as 584 miles away from the center of the earth. Never before had human beings built a rocket that could fly above the earth's atmosphere. The Russians named their satellite *Sputnik*, meaning "fellow traveler of the Earth."

Because of the success of *Sputnik*, Americans decided to step up their own space program. In 1958 the United States government set up the National Aeronautics and Space Administration (NASA). All the space research groups in the country, including the one at Edwards, became part of NASA. NASA's purpose was to catch up to the Soviet Union in building rockets.

After the Soviets launched *Sputnik I* on October 4, 1957, the United States began to accelerate its space program. This replica of the first satellite is displayed at the United Nations Building in New York City.

Soon United States satellites were being sent into orbit, and people were being trained as astronauts. Neil was eager to participate in the great new adventure of space exploration. While working as a NASA test pilot, he volunteered for the astronaut program. But competition for the few available openings was tough. Applicants had to be jet pilots who had completed at least 1,000 hours of flying time. They had to meet several other requirements as well, including height, weight, age, and health. Applicants also had to have a college degree.

Neil Armstrong (right) was among the second group of astronauts to be selected for the space program. Most of them participated in both the Gemini and the Apollo missions.

Neil did not think his chances for becoming an astronaut were very good. The people who were already in the training program had begun their careers in the military, but Neil was a civilian. So when his application was accepted in 1962, Neil was both surprised and pleased. He became the first civilian ever admitted to the astronaut program.

The Armstrongs were sad to leave their beautiful mountain home, but they were excited about moving to El Lago, Texas. El Lago was a quiet community where many astronauts and their families lived. It was close to the NASA Manned Spacecraft Center in Houston, where Neil would spend the next two years training to be an astronaut.

A view of NASA's Manned Spacecraft Center in the 1960s

The training program proved to be difficult. Neil and the other new men put in many hours of classroom work. They studied outer space and the movements of the sun, moon, and stars. They learned about rockets and how to pilot a space capsule. They also were trained to navigate alone in space with the aid of stars and computers.

Besides classroom work, the new astronauts underwent rugged physical training. They had to accustom their bodies to high pressure, weightlessness, and other conditions they would find in space.

While Neil was busy with his training, NASA was making world headlines. Only three years after it was formed, NASA launched the first American, Alan B. Shepard, into space. Shortly after Shepard's flight, President John F. Kennedy made a famous speech. "Space is open to us now," he said. He urged Americans to join together in an effort to put a person on the moon by 1970.

To carry out President Kennedy's plan, the government established three separate space projects, Mercury, Gemini, and Apollo. Each project was more advanced than the one before it and came closer to the ultimate goal—landing on the moon.

The last Mercury flight leaves the launch pad on May 15, 1963.

The Mercury Project lasted from May 1961 to May 1963. Six tiny Mercury capsules were launched during this two-year period. Each capsule carried one person.

The purpose of these six flights was to learn how human beings would react to the new environment of outer space.

In the Gemini Project, 10 flights were made between 1965 and 1966. The Gemini capsule was three times as large as the Mercury one, with room for two people. The Gemini Project was designed to test the effects of long space flights on human beings and to teach astronauts how to fly their capsules without using computer control from the ground.

The Apollo Project began in 1968 and ended in 1975. The 12 Apollo craft launched during this time were twice the size of the Gemini capsule and carried three crew members. The purpose of this project was by far the most exciting: to land human beings on the moon.

In 1966 NASA was preparing to launch *Gemini 8*. The mission of this capsule was to perform the first space docking in history. This meant that *Gemini 8* would connect, or dock, with a second spacecraft that was already in orbit. But NASA still had to choose a commander for *Gemini 8*. Neil had just finished his intensive training and was given charge of the historic flight.

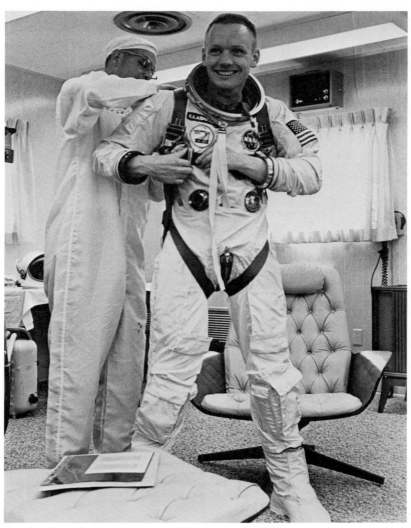

Gemini 8 command pilot Neil Armstrong suits up for his first space flight.

Armstrong (left) and fellow astronaut David R. Scott prepare to board *Gemini 8*, which was launched by a Titan II rocket (opposite).

Gemini 8 lifted off from the launching pad at Cape Kennedy, Florida, on March 16, 1966. Neil and his crewman, David R. Scott, traveled across 105,000 miles of space to reach the orbiting spacecraft.

For the first time, Neil saw what the world looked like from outer space. In many ways its shape resembled a schoolroom globe. The oceans were a vivid blue. Snowy white clouds hid parts of the continents.

Gemini 8 (foreground) prepares to dock with the smaller, unmanned spacecraft shown in the distance.

Space itself was black and empty. Stars seemed much brighter and nearer than they did from earth.

Armstrong and Scott caught up to the orbiting spacecraft high above the South Atlantic Ocean. Now it was Neil's job to steer the nose of *Gemini 8* into the docking collar of the other vehicle. Carefully he eased his craft forward. The two connected perfectly.

"As easy as parking a car," he radioed back to earth.

The locked vehicles drifted over the Atlantic Ocean, Africa, and the Indian Ocean. Then something went wrong. The two crafts began to pitch and spin wildly. Swiftly and skillfully, Armstrong detached the Gemini capsule from the other craft, which floated off into space. But pretty soon *Gemini 8* began spinning faster than ever. It was turning at the rate of one revolution per second! Radio contact between earth and *Gemini 8* crackled and faded.

The NASA crew back on earth waited breathlessly. Was *Gemini 8* lost in space? Then Armstrong's voice came through crisp and clear. He had succeeded in steadying the craft. His piloting skill had saved them. Armstrong then guided *Gemini 8* to an emergency splashdown in the Pacific Ocean. People everywhere breathed a sigh of relief.

While NASA completed the next two flights in the Gemini Project, Neil went back to test flying. Two years later he had another close call when a jet trainer he was flying crashed. Fortunately he was able to parachute to safety.

The first flight in the Apollo Project was *Apollo 7*, launched on October 11, 1968 (opposite). *Apollo 8*, the powerful 363-foot high Saturn V launch vehicle (above) was used for the first moon flight.

Finally it was time for the last of the three great space projects. The Apollo Project, which began in 1968, sent out four exploratory flights. The last one brought human beings to within nine miles of the moon's surface.

The next craft, *Apollo 11*, would make the historic moon landing. Two of the three people chosen for the *Apollo 11* crew would be the first to walk on the moon. On January 9, 1969, NASA announced the crew. The pilots would be Edwin E. Aldrin, Jr., and Michael Collins. Neil Armstrong was named the commander.

In the months before the flight, the astronauts were kept very busy. They studied moon maps and photographs, spent hours learning about rocks, photography, and weather, and practiced working the controls of their spacecraft. In special laboratories built to resemble the surface of the moon, the astronauts learned to move about in their bulky space suits. Each suit cost $100,000 and had to be sturdily built so tiny space particles called meteoroids could not puncture it. The suit had its own supply of air, water, and electricity. It also carried a fan and refrigeration unit to deal with sharp changes of temperature.

The last 10 days before the launch, the astronauts seldom left their crew quarters. They saw few people because doctors feared they might pick up some disease. Even a sore throat would mean delaying the flight for a month.

The three *Apollo II* astronauts — (left to right) Collins, Armstrong, and Aldrin — in their space suits in front of a model of the lunar landing module (LM) that would land Armstrong and Aldrin on the moon

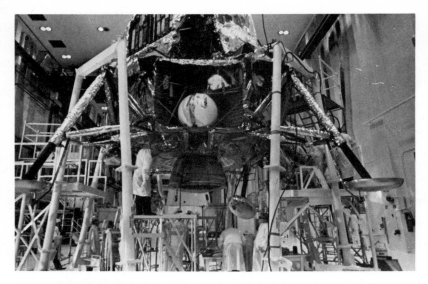

While the astronauts practiced for their flight, the various parts of their spacecraft were being built and tested — the lunar landing module (top), the first stage of the Saturn V launch rocket (bottom), and the command and service modules (opposite).

INTEGRATED
TEST STAND
Nº 1

Commander Armstrong practices for the moon landing inside the lunar module simulator (opposite). In the photograph above, he is shown descending the ladder of the simulator.

As launch day approached, excitement grew. People from all over the world arrived at Cape Kennedy, including reporters, mayors, tourists, students, and senators. Thousands of cars lined the highways. One million people had gathered to witness this historic event!

Collins (left) and Armstrong eat breakfast on the morning of their historic moon flight.

On the morning of July 16, 1969, Commander Armstrong and his crew mates rose before dawn. They ate a hearty breakfast of steak, scrambled eggs, toast, orange juice, and coffee. Then they put on their white space suits, and a truck drove them to the launching pad. An elevator lifted them high into the air, to the very top of the huge Saturn rocket. This rocket was as tall as a 36-floor building. From here the men could see for miles. They saw sand dunes and palm trees, hundreds of boats floating in nearby rivers, and the sparkling blue Atlantic Ocean in the distance.

When it was time, Neil Armstrong, Edwin "Buzz" Aldrin, and Mike Collins boarded the spacecraft. The heavy outer door of the capsule was then sealed shut. The countdown began. "Ten...nine...eight ...seven...six...five...four...three...two...one ...zero!" Millions of people around the world waited tensely. Suddenly orange flames and clouds of smoke shot up around the rocket. There was a mighty roar, and the ground trembled and shook for miles around.

"Lift-off! We have lift-off!" came Neil's voice from within the spacecraft. The Saturn rocket shuddered. Ever so slowly it rose into the air. Then it rapidly picked up speed. After 10 years of preparation, the voyage to the moon had begun!

The Saturn rocket, also called a launch vehicle, provided the power to send *Apollo 11* to the moon. The rocket had three stages, and each one sent the spacecraft further into outer space. The first stage fueled the lift-off and then dropped off two and a half minutes later. The second stage carried the Apollo craft 116 miles above the earth and dropped off six and a half minutes later. At this point, the third stage sent the spacecraft into orbit around the earth and then to the moon.

The spacecraft had three sections, a command module, a service module, and a lunar module. On the way to the moon, these three sections went through a series of changes. First, the command module, called *Columbia*, and the service module separated from the lunar module, called *Eagle*, and the third stage of the Saturn rocket. Then the command and service modules turned around and docked with the lunar module. Finally, the third stage dropped off, and *Apollo* 11 was on its own. Behind it the earth was a beautiful blue green sphere against the blackness.

The journey to the moon lasted four days. During that time the astronauts had many important chores to perform. They had calculations to make and instruments to watch. They also broadcast color TV pictures to viewers on earth. These were the sharpest, clearest TV pictures ever sent from outer space.

Each crew member had a specific task. Mike Collins was navigator and pilot. His job was to fly the crew

from the earth to the moon and back again. Buzz Aldrin was the expert on systems and machines. But Neil Armstrong had the most exciting job of all. He would fly the *Eagle* down to the surface of the moon and lead the expedition outside the craft.

The gray moon seemed to grow larger and larger as *Apollo 11* got closer. The astronauts could see the moon's round shape clearly. "It seemed almost as if it were showing us its roundness, its similarity in shape to our earth, in a sort of welcome," Armstrong said. "I was sure that it would be a hospitable host. It had been awaiting its first visitors for a long time."

The men saw that many areas of the moon were covered with large holes, or craters. Other areas were dark and smooth, like vast oceans. Astronomers called these areas "seas," even though there is no water on the moon. The seas are nothing more than dry plains.

Now it was time for the final preparations before reaching the moon. The spacecraft went into orbit around the moon. Armstrong and Aldrin crawled through the narrow passage from the *Columbia* to the *Eagle*, the module that would land them on the moon. Collins remained in the *Columbia*. Then the *Eagle* separated from the command and service

The moon's surface as seen from *Apollo II*. The round hole in
the center of the photograph is a crater, 50 miles wide.

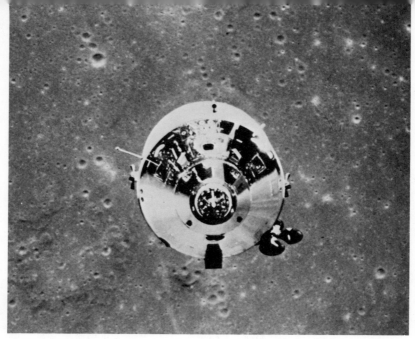

A photograph of the command module taken from inside the lunar module as the lunar module heads toward the moon

modules. "The *Eagle* has wings," Armstrong reported to Mission Control back on earth.

While Collins continued circling the moon in the *Columbia*, Armstrong and Aldrin began their nine-mile descent. If something were to go wrong now, it could spell disaster. One of the *Eagle's* spindly legs could snap. A boulder or a steep slope could cause the craft to fall onto its side. If that happened, the two explorers would be unable to lift off again. They would be stranded on the moon.

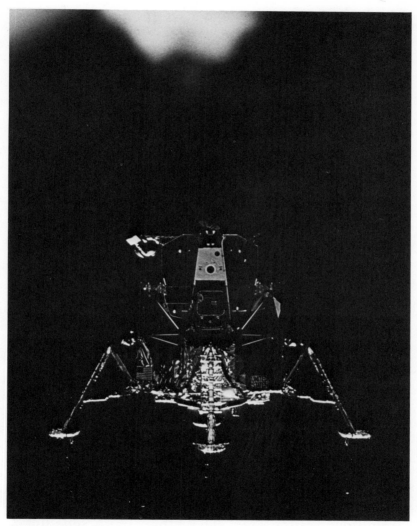

Astronaut Collins in the command module took this photograph of the lunar module with Armstrong and Aldrin aboard.

The moonscape rushed below them. A computer guided the *Eagle* toward its selected landing site near the Sea of Tranquility. Scientists had selected this site because it looked smooth and safe. But when Armstrong looked out the window, he was startled. The landing site was actually a crater as wide as a football field and very deep. And the ground wasn't smooth at all—it was covered with huge rocks!

Quickly Armstrong took control of the *Eagle* from the computer. Guiding the craft by hand, he skimmed over the boulders, looking for flat ground. Flashing red lights warned that fuel was low. Gently he lowered the *Eagle* to the surface. Armstrong's calm voice radioed back, "The *Eagle* has landed."

At Mission Control people started breathing again. In about 30 seconds the *Eagle's* fuel supply would have been gone. One control man turned to another and said, "I think he's the greatest pilot in the whole world."

Armstrong and Aldrin checked all systems on the *Eagle* to be sure nothing had been damaged in landing. They got everything ready for a quick takeoff in case something went wrong. Then they were scheduled to take a nap, but they were too excited! They requested permission to begin exploring the moon, and Mission Control agreed.

Neil Armstrong climbed down the ladder of the *Eagle* and became the first human being to step onto the moon. "That's one small step for a man, one giant leap for mankind," he said. His words, broadcast over radio and TV to listeners and viewers the world over, would never be forgotten.

As he began to explore the moon, Armstrong saw a desolate area. Rocks and craters littered an empty landscape. Nothing grew at all. The sky appeared to be dark at all times. "But it's very pretty out here," Armstrong radioed back.

There is no air on the moon to make the sky look blue, and no wind or water. Since the moon is unprotected from the sun's deadly rays, the temperature reaches wide extremes. At its hottest it climbs to 250°F. (121°C.) At its coldest it plunges to 280° below zero (-138°C.)

The moon's gravity is much less than that of earth. With full gear Armstrong weighed 360 pounds on earth. On the moon he weighed only 60 pounds. This meant that walking on the moon would be very different from walking on earth. Would Armstrong be able to balance? If he fell and ripped his suit, it could mean sudden death. But Armstrong reported, "It's actually no trouble to walk around."

Soon Aldrin left the *Eagle* and joined Armstrong on the surface. TV viewers a quarter of a million miles away watched the two men walk with slow, bounding strides. After they were used to moving about in very little gravity, the men settled down to work.

Armstrong photographs partner Aldrin as Aldrin leaves the spacecraft to complete a series of experiments.

Aldrin takes a sample of lunar soil. The two astronauts spent approximately 2 hours and 20 minutes outside of their spacecraft and collected 48 pounds of surface material to bring back to earth.

In the next two and a half hours they did many things. They planted an American flag and set up TV cameras. They took photographs, gathered moon rocks, and performed several scientific experiments.

Finally Aldrin climbed back aboard the *Eagle*. Armstrong remained outside to collect a few more rocks, which scientists would study back on earth. Then he climbed back into the lunar module. The two astronauts had left large footprints on the moon's soft surface during their work. Because of the moon's environment, those prints might remain undisturbed for hundreds of years.

The next morning Armstrong and Aldrin prepared to blast off. The lower half of the *Eagle* would serve as a launching pad for the upper part.

The rockets fired, lifting the two astronauts away from the moon. Miles above the surface Armstrong docked the *Columbia*, and they rejoined Collins in the command module. The *Eagle* had completed its task, so it was abandoned.

The ascent stage of the lunar module moves toward the command module for docking.

Four days later the *Columbia* returned to earth. It arched gracefully over Australia and the Coral Sea, splashing down in the Pacific Ocean. Within an hour, Armstrong and his crew were hoisted into a helicopter. They flew to the U.S.S. *Hornet*, a battleship 11 miles away. There they were greeted by the president of the United States, Richard M. Nixon.

"Congratulations, Neil, Buzz, and Mike," the president said. "The response to your accomplishment has been tremendous. In Washington we have received messages and greetings from more than 100 foreign governments. They come from emperors and presidents, prime ministers and kings. You have helped bring the peoples of the world closer together. You have taught man how to reach for the stars."

For the next 18 days, the astronauts were kept in isolation to make sure that no deadly, unknown germs had been brought back from outer space. Most scientists believed the moon's environment was too hostile for such germs to exist, but they wanted to make certain there was no danger.

Finally the isolation period ended. Armstrong, Aldrin, and Collins were honored in a ticker-tape parade in New York City. Not since aviator Charles

Thousands cheer the three astronauts during a ticker-tape parade down Broadway in New York City.

Lindbergh flew across the Atlantic had anyone been given such a hero's welcome. The astronauts also took part in other parades and celebrations. The president awarded each the Medal of Freedom, the highest United States civilian award anyone can receive. Later the men visited 22 nations. Everywhere they were greeted by thousands of people.

When Armstrong returned home, he was a hero. The street where his parents lived in Wapakoneta, Ohio, was renamed Neil Armstrong Drive. The people of his hometown proudly celebrated Neil Armstrong days. And the little airport where he took his first flying lessons was now called the Neil Armstrong Airport.

But even as a hero, Armstrong remained quiet and shy. People joked that he only showed enthusiasm when speaking of aeronautics or flying. It was true that flying was still his first love.

In 1970, a year after the historic flight to the moon, Armstrong resigned from NASA. He wanted to make room for younger astronauts, and he wanted time to be with his wife, Janet, and his sons, Ricky and Mark.

In 1971 Armstrong moved back to Ohio. He taught aeronautical engineering at the University of Cincinnati until 1980 and worked for the Chrysler Corporation from 1979 to 1981. In 1980 Armstrong became board chairman of Cardwell International, a manufacturer of oil field equipment in Lebanon, Ohio. He also served on the board of directors of several firms, including Gates Learjet and United Airlines.

In his spare time, Armstrong pursues his favorite

hobby—gliding. He spends many peaceful hours soaring silently through the blue midwestern skies in his sailplane. Sometimes an early moon might be floating with him in the sky, a moon whose surface is now marked by human footprints. Above these footprints on that lonely moonscape is a bronze plaque left by the first moon explorers. The plaque was signed by Neil Armstrong, the *Apollo 11* crew, and the president of the United States. It reads:

HERE MEN FROM THE PLANET EARTH
FIRST SET FOOT UPON THE MOON
JULY 1969, A. D.
WE CAME IN PEACE FOR ALL MANKIND

NEIL A. ARMSTRONG
ASTRONAUT

MICHAEL COLLINS
ASTRONAUT

EDWIN E. ALDRIN, JR.
ASTRONAUT

RICHARD NIXON
PRESIDENT, UNITED STATES OF AMERICA

After centuries of dreaming, human beings had at last reached the moon. And Neil Armstrong, space pioneer, had been part of that great adventure from the beginning.

UNITED STATES MANNED SPACE FLIGHTS
THROUGH PROJECT APOLLO

MISSION AND SPACECRAFT	CREW MEMBERS	DATE(S) OF MISSION AND LENGTH OF TIME IN SPACE	NUMBER OF REVOLUTIONS (ORBITS) AROUND EARTH
Mercury 3 *Freedom 7*	Alan B. Shepard, Jr.	May 5, 1961 15 minutes	suborbital
Mercury 4 *Liberty Bell 7*	Virgil I. Grissom	July 21, 1961 16 minutes	suborbital
Mercury 6 *Friendship 7*	John H. Glenn, Jr.	February 20, 1962 4 hours, 55 minutes	3

Mercury 7 *Aurora 7*	M. Scott Carpenter	May 24, 1962 4 hours, 56 minutes	3
Mercury 8 *Sigma 7*	Walter M. Schirra, Jr.	October 3, 1962 9 hours, 13 minutes	6
Mercury 9 *Faith 7*	L. Gordon Cooper, Jr.	May 15-16, 1963 1 day, 10 hours, 20 minutes	22
Gemini 3 *Molly Brown*	Virgil I. Grissom John M. Young	March 23, 1965 4 hours, 53 minutes	3
Gemini 4	James A. McDivitt Edward H. White II	June 3-7, 1965 4 days, 1 hour, 56 minutes	62
Gemini 5	L. Gordon Cooper, Jr. Charles Conrad, Jr.	August 21-29, 1965 7 days, 22 hours, 56 minutes	120
Gemini 7	Frank Borman James A. Lovell, Jr.	December 4-18, 1965 13 days, 18 hours, 35 minutes	206
Gemini 6	Walter M. Schirra, Jr. Thomas P. Stafford	December 15-16, 1965 1 day, 1 hour, 51 minutes	16
Gemini 8	**Neil A. Armstrong David R. Scott**	**March 16, 1966 10 hours, 41 minutes**	**7**
Gemini 9	Thomas P. Stafford Eugene A Cernan	June 3-6, 1966 3 days, 21 minutes	44
Gemini 10	John W. Young Michael Collins	July 18-21, 1966 2 days, 22 hours, 47 minutes	43
Gemini 11	Charles Conrad, Jr. Richard F. Gordon, Jr.	September 12-15, 1966 2 days, 23 hours, 17 minutes	44
Gemini 12	James A. Lovell, Jr. Edwin E. Aldrin, Jr.	November 11-15, 1966 3 days, 22 hours, 35 minutes	59

(continued)

Apollo 7 (CSM only)	Walter M. Schirra, Jr. Donn F. Eisle R. Walter Cunningham	October 11-22, 1968 10 days, 20 hours	163
Apollo 8 (CSM only)	Frank Borman James A. Lovell, Jr. William A. Anders	December 21-27, 1968 6 days, 3 hours, 1 minute	10†
Apollo 9 *Gumdrop* (CSM)* *Spider* (LM)**	James A. McDivitt David R. Scott Russell L. Schweickart	March 3-13, 1969 10 days, 1 hour, 1 minute	151
Apollo 10 *Charlie Brown* (CSM) *Snoopy* (LM)	Thomas P. Stafford John W. Young Eugene A. Cernan	May 18-26, 1969 8 days, 3 minutes	31†
Apollo 11 ***Columbia* (CSM)** ***Eagle* (LM)**	**Neil A. Armstrong** **Michael Collins** **Edwin E. Aldrin, Jr.**	**July 16-24, 1969** **8 days, 3 hours,** **19 minutes**	**30†**
Apollo 12 *Yankee Clipper* (CSM) *Intrepid* (LM)	Charles Conrad, Jr. Richard F. Gordon Alan L. Bean	November 14-24, 1969 10 days, 4 hours, 36 minutes	45†
Apollo 13 *Odyssey* (CSM) *Aquarius* (LM)	James A. Lovell, Jr. John L. Swigert, Jr. Fred W. Haise, Jr.	April 11-17, 1970 5 days, 22 hours, 55 minutes	
Apollo 14 *Kitty Hawk* (CSM) *Antares* (LM)	Alan B. Shepard, Jr. Stuart A. Roosa Edgar D. Mitchell	January 31- February 9, 1971 9 days, 2 minutes	34†
Apollo 15 *Endeavor* (CSM) *Falcon* (LM)	David R. Scott Alfred M. Worden James B. Irwin	July 26- August 7, 1971 12 days, 7 hours, 12 minutes	74†
Apollo 16 *Casper* (CSM) *Orion* (LM)	John W. Young Thomas K. Mattingly II Charles M. Duke, Jr.	April 16-27, 1972 11 days, 1 hour, 51 minutes	64†
Apollo 17 *America* (CSM) *Challenger* (LM)	Eugene A. Cernan Ronald E. Evans Harrison H. Schmitt	December 7-19, 1972 12 days, 13 hours, 52 minutes	75†

Command and Service Modules
**Lunar Module*
†*moon orbits*

921
Ar

Westman, Paul

Neil Armstrong,
space pioneer

c.1

DATE DUE